Heart of the Broken World

Jeff Weddle

Nixes Mate Books
Allston, Massachusetts

Copyright © 2017 Jeff Weddle

Book design by d'Entremont
Cover photograph from the collection of Lauren Leja

All rights reserved. This book or any portion thereof may not be reproduced or used in any manner whatsoever without the express written permission of the publisher except for the use of brief quotations in a book review or scholarly journal.

Grateful acknowledgment is made to the following, where some of these poems previously appeared: *Alien Buddha; Belinda Subramann's Gypsy Art Show; Chiron Review; Journal of Kentucky Studies; Nihilistic Review; Pressure Press Presents;* and *The Wingnut Brigade*.

ISBN 978-0-9991882-8-6

Nixes Mate Books
POBox 1179
Allston, MA 02134
nixesmate.pub/books

Always for Jill

Contents

Heart of the Broken World	1
What We Can Expect	3
Drowning Alone	5
One with Everything	6
It will be Later Still	7
The Good News	8
Same as Anybody	10
In the Beginning was	12
The Price of Creation	13
Kaja	14
Most Important Meal of the Day	16
Night Music	17
Moments Persist	18
Gus at the End of the World	19
But Then Again	20
Jay's Bed	22
I Like to Think You Killed a Man	24
All the Roads	26
After	27
Cabin Witch	28
Time out of Mind	30

That First Affair	32
Bouquet	34
Green Light	35
Anodyne Night	36
Careless Grace	37
An Ordinary Story	38
Vicious Love	40
Big Dance	41
Lost Baggage	44
Summer of Love	45
Last Call	48
It's True	50

Heart of the Broken World

Heart of the Broken World

do not fear
your soft secrets
the heart
of the broken world
requires them
and your unknown love
and the balance
of lipstick
on your cheek
with the empty nights
to come
and the history
of all things
do not fear
this tender spark
it is your one true moment
of grace

What We Can Expect

Lost love or no love
or love betrayed
empty promises broken
on the dirty sheets
of an October morning
lies made without regret
dying dogs and indifferent cats
a universe empty of proper conversation
poems that smell like piss
and sound like noise
dismissed valor
long days at bad jobs
and the rent takes everything
children without chance
children drunk and no one cares
children who remember your darkness
bad teeth
bad heart
bad intentions
misplaced interest
turds in the soup bowl
and dinner can't wait

rusted locks and lost keys
forlorn rags
grapes stolen from supermarket plenty
and the blades the blades the blades
screams and silence
everybody's story

Drowning Alone

the walls are liquid
and we are drowning alone
all the lovely women
naked on screens of various device
and we are drowning alone
and we are tired and frightened
most of us are sad
those who bag your groceries
are defeated
and those who preach Jesus
are defeated
and all the insurance agents
and dog catchers
and narcs
are defeated
your teachers
are defeated
and your heroes
and the pilots of aircraft
and the stewardesses
and all the passengers
and the railroad engineers

everyone murdered
all of us
the walls are liquid and lovely poison
and we are drowning alone
even the lovely naked women
on the screens
oh, unknown
oh, lost
I would take your hand
I would take your hand

One with Everything

I am practically content,
like dying neon
in a bar
of warm embrace,
and can feel
my questions
in the way
the flowers
hold still
when they know
we are watching.
Like them, the dance
is all we are allowed.

It will be Later Still

We are brittle,
brown sticks in a basket.
The man who could once
stick his heel through four inches of wood,
his knuckles through three,
is now more belly than brave,
bald head shining like a beacon to decay.
It goes so fast, that thing, that moment
that seemed, just then, eternal.
The great, bellowing joke –
things gifted and taken away.
Nothing pays the final mortgage
and aging hands finally cease
being hands at all.
There is a photograph:
Young men flying at each other
in fierce grace,
everything focused in the smallest moment,
unreal even then, fluid, draining as it has
to this couch, this pen, this quiet morning
of my old refrigerator humming
and light, subdued, dancing beyond the blinds.

The Good News

Everything is holy
Even the killing of innocents
Even starvation is holy
Even hatred
Even the razor on the flesh
Even that is holy
Holy is the awful fire
Holy is the sum and the total
Holy is how days become night
Holy is the young girl broken
and the boy left bleeding
Holy is the despair of the aged
Holy is the mother church
Holy is this game
Our Father, oh Father
Holy is thy plan
Holy is thy bondage upon the earth
Come blast and horror
Come disease
Come heartbreak and absent love
Come holy
Come holy

Come hard days without end
Come pristine desert
Come the whip
Come thorns
Come holy
Take this cup from me
I am sick with it and it is filled with bile
Holy be thy name

Same as Anybody

Jesus liked to party
with the witches
from lower Duval
He managed flowers
at the children's hotel
as lonesome and unglamorous
a job as there is
and sometimes
He made the flowers bloom
out of season
and sometimes
He stole a bouquet for Lucy
the witch He loved most well
the one with a glass eye
and no illusions
and Lucy, no surprise,
always tossed the flowers
in the gutter
so she might
enjoy them
another time
Jesus almost understood
but women are tricky

for anyone
even the son
of the great I Am
and maybe for Him
most of all
Jesus lived
in a constant war
against chaos
and chaos generally
kicked His ass
that's why
He climbed up on that cross
it was consensual
and Jesus went home
as He always does
and Lucy wept
and gathered up all her flowers
and cast them to the heavens
and that is how we got
the stars

In the Beginning was

She awoke
and for just one second
remembered her dream
remembered that
it had come to her
the word
the single word
that gave her true visions
that created her in that moment
the word the entire world
had forgotten
and then the dream was gone
in the way of dreams
the word gone with it
leaving only a gash
where happiness
almost might have been
you are wise
so you understand:
this is grace
this is as lucky as it gets

The Price of Creation

The cost of this poem
is one large coffee mug
gone crashing to the floor
a big round mug
comfortable in my hand
and bought with my family
on a happy day
in Alaska
and the coffee it held
still piping hot
and the memories it contained
and the moment
years from now
I would have held it
while talking to my son or daughter
grown into someone
I don't yet know
asking them in the way of prayer
to recall some dear time
to please remember our days

Kaja

She felt she was a saint
maybe Christ
and though the burden was hard
having no choice
she carried it well.

Her small room had light and heat
only a few hours of the day
but she had her typewriter and paper
and there were always parties
in the way of artists and writers
and there was wine and smoke
and she enjoyed long walks
in the cold Paris evenings
bundled in sweaters
and the expectation of happiness
coming sometime soon.

Love was always available for a moment
even for a plain girl like her
but not the love
for which she had crossed an ocean.

That love had casually fled to Africa
with a young beauty
even before she arrived
and was, in any case, impossible.

She had visions of the divine
and wrote every day for hours
and kept the pages safe in big trunks
which she was certain
the world would someday know.

What became of her is a mystery
and the trunks are long vanished
but maybe she is in heaven
at the right hand of God.
This is my prayer for her blessing.

Most Important Meal of the Day

I had a poem in my head just now
as I was fixing my breakfast
a skillet filled three times
with pancakes
whole grain and essential
pancakes with too much butter
and what was left
of the maple syrup in the pantry
everything warm on my tongue
and supplicant
I had this poem in my head
had it worked out word by word
a decent poem I suppose
now gone
as I sit here eating these pancakes
not a bit of the poem remaining
but the pancakes
are fluffy and good
and I decide
as though it were true
this is the thing that matters

Night Music

Folding laundry
to *Rubber Soul*,
the wife asleep,
the children tucked away.
"In My Life"
hits me like
a whispered embrace.
All the years
meet in this moment
of boy's jeans
and little girl's socks
and dozens of small things
Jill wears and tosses aside.
I cry too easily
not just now
but sometimes.

Moments Persist

A child's shirt
blue and discarded
I retrieve it
from her bedroom floor
a floor so littered with toys
and little girl treasures
I can barely find footing
treasures whose magic
I, being old,
can only imagine.
I hang the shirt
neatly in her closet.
In ten years
she will be gone
from this house,
but today
she is still mine,
eight years old,
all sparkle and demand,
and I forgive her
everything.

Gus at the End of the World

At the exact moment
the world ended –
well, a hundredth
of a millisecond previous,
if you want to be exact –
the boy raised his plastic sword
in pure joy
and his father
snapped a photograph.

But Then Again

That green sweater
held her body
like fortune
while he fooled
with the camera.

"Don't point that at me,"
she said, because perhaps
it would steal her soul,
or maybe give him
the wrong idea.

Just a boy and a girl
lingering by rocks and water.

And some might say
they were us,
and that might be untrue,
but who can remember that far?

And she had hair like smoked honey,
and the sky was in her eyes.

Let's say it was autumn,
the best of the seasons,
and happy.

Jay's Bed

More than the rest of it
I have tried to make this bed
my own. The couch and
barstools fit nicely
on the floor though the
reshuffling of both has left
ruts in the ancient wax.

I use the pots and pans
and silverware and each
morning my one bowl
holds two helpings of
corn flakes. But the bed
sits in that other room
and says to me: *I am
given in trust.* And to her:
Do not forget me.

Those nights we lie upon it
are blackout and amnesia.
In the mornings we stretch
and kiss and move quickly

to the kitchen. In that room,
little as there is,
I own almost everything.

I Like to Think You Killed a Man

I remember every detail
but some things I keep
to myself.

It's not the way I want it
but you don't like to hear
and no one else
gives a damn.

Shall we agree
that the Germans wore gray
and you wore blue?

That's a way to laugh things off
and laughing is for the best
right?

Sure it is.

As always
the usual suspects
know nothing

and awkward goodbyes
like train stations in the rain
linger in dreams
and in the bloody bandages
we call art.

Someday you'll understand
but I never make plans
that far in advance.

All the Roads

You are companion
of my dreams
my most intimate mystery
and you have forgotten
all the things I cherish
this life must be kind
to some
or there wouldn't be
all those happy songs
but who they are
the happy ones
has not been revealed
only these dreams
which hold me
and I am sure
I will never
understand my life
beautiful one
or the dreams
that bleed me
or why you are
so far away

After

now
        clothed
more naked
           than before
unfasten the lock
the sun
           washes in
              and
your eyes are so
                    blue

Cabin Witch

little red cabin
with wasps
in the walls
there's a witch
in there forever
and her spells
echo past
the addictions
and death
of friends
and family
the betrayals
and lost hope
all the bad life
that came after
the blessings
of that red cabin
and the wasps
we killed
with hairspray
and matches
blessings
like that
acid night

when the dogs
encircled us
and, possessed,
bit through
the cans
to drink
our beer
as the stars
did things
no other people
ever saw
there's a witch
in there forever
and you'd call her
a poet
but she remains
so much more
our lady of the cabin
immortal
and damned
fucked hard
shining
like nobody's business

Time out of Mind

all at once
I saw you old
a flash of mind
though I have
not really seen you
in thirty years
and you were thin
and wrinkled
in an unfashionable
cloth coat
and in this flash of mind
a child mocked you
for being ancient
and you wanted to tell her
what she would never believe:
the two of us in a bathtub
fucking and immortal
the way we thought
we would always be
and then you were gone
and I wondered if you
were alive or dead

or if you
ever thought of me
or that bath
or marveled
as I sometimes do
that we ever
said goodbye

That First Affair

It was a rusted out Buick, too corny, yes,
but that's the truth of the thing, and you
were twelve. I was eleven and scared
but I loved you, and you held my hand.
I can still feel the sweat of our palms
as we sat in the front seat of that old car
and you said the words,
asked me if I wanted to kiss you.
I said no, because I was eleven and scared,
and you got mad, I guess, because you hit me
and ran away. I sat there for hours, waiting
for you to come back, but you never did,
and the sun went down and later my mother
whipped me for staying out till she was frantic.
And after that we never sat together in old cars
or held hands or spoke much, really.
I saw in the paper today that your daughter
had a child. Darling, you are too young
to be a grandmother, and I am too old,
too scared even now to tell you any of this.
The truth is that I never left that Buick, not ever,
not even now. I know that waiting is foolish.

I just wanted to say congratulations, to wish you well,
to say you should cherish all your babies,
to wave goodbye in the dark.

Bouquet

the subject was roses
roses like the ones
I bought at that florist
on the corner
by the German bakery
the roses I gave you
for no reason
and you took them
confused and glad
the last time we met
that October afternoon
in the rain

Green Light

she was in the corner
reading Gatsby
and we were all drowned
and stupid with youth
the play of beauty
on a page was everything
and she was in the dark corner
reading Gatsby
as the guests danced
and drank in the light
she was unaware, golden
sitting in the corner reading Gatsby

Anodyne Night

she shuffled twice
and offered me the cut
and I had been watching her
for so long that my coffee
was already cold
and ready for the drain
so I swapped it
for the pinot noir
in a white paper cup
and watched
as she nibbled a cookie
just to the edge of a big raisin
and slid it back onto the tray
that's when I saw
her hair was darker
than the vault of heaven
and twice as lush
and all at once I understood
the whole world

this is what beauty is

Careless Grace

Some day if you're lucky
you might see a woman
in a red t-shirt and blue shorts
walking through a parking lot
on a hot summer day
a beautiful woman
of raven hair and careless grace
and though you might see her
for only a moment
before the world turns an inch
and she's gone
that's fine
visions are not meant to last
only to inspire and fade
and remain with you
in small and fundamental ways
like the smell of warm biscuits and honey
or the wisp of a good dream
or the memory of something
that never happened
but maybe should have

An Ordinary Story

He decided she was just a fever dream,
night sweats and delusion.
There being no cure for dreams but waking,
he set about to do so.
He drank a lot of coffee,
but coffee reminded him of her chestnut hair.
Someone said exercise is good for what ails you,
but calisthenics just made him think
of how his heart raced when she was near.
So, he took himself to a hospital,
the kind that cures fever dreams,
and after a respectable time,
they told him he was cured.
And so he was, until the day
he walked into the grocery store,
and there she stood,
bending over the russet potatoes,
and scratching the back of her neck
with the third finger of her left hand.
A week later, his landlady found him
hanging in his closet from a red necktie.
These words, on neatly folded legal paper,

were all he left behind:
"My mind was ever weak,
and there was never skin so soft."
She was back at the grocery that Thursday,
like always, her regular shopping day,
because they doubled coupons on Thursdays,
and she never tired of flirting with Jimbo,
the guy who ran the seafood counter.
And she remained happy, and life went on.
Months later, someone told her
a man she once knew had died,
but, for the life of her,
she couldn't remember a thing about him,
not even the shape of his face.

Vicious Love

you see girls walking down the street
admire fine buttocks legs breasts
think, know, how they would be
but not for you
wonder about the one the one the one
who's not for you, either
and she appears
as if by magic
from across the street
and comes and talks talks talks
and how does she get in touch at your new address?
crazy men madmen and insane men
know what it is
know how it is
there is no cure
there is no cure
she'll always be out there somewhere
out there away from you
but somehow finding her way back
bringing cold salt water to your place in hell

Big Dance

I want to dance with Emma Goldman
across the Brooklyn Bridge, 3 a.m.
and the world on fire
and be struck by dangerous winds
and hold the beating heart of time
and love with the ferocity of a bomb
shattering a bourgeois window.

I want to dance with Emma Goldman
as the streets run alive with free men and women
and have no more need for blood
only poetry and bread and art.

I want to dance with Emma Goldman
in the great Midwestern cornfields
and the coal mines of home Appalachia
in broad shouldered Chicago
in the dying main streets of dying American towns
in beleaguered New Orleans
across the living dream of the Golden Gate Bridge.

And as I dance with Emma Goldman
the tiny, frightened policemen
these hateful oafs
will have no place
their murderous guns transformed
to the hearts of children.

I want to dance with Michael Brown
with Treyvon Martin
with Sandra Bland
the Charleston Massacre Nine
the Sandy Hook children
and all the victims
of horrid American madness.

I want to dance with Emma Goldman
while the bosses gladly pay a living wage
while teachers are allowed to teach truth
and not the lies of preachers and corporate thugs.

I want to dance with Emma Goldman.
I want to dance.
I want to dance.
I want to goddamn dance
in a world where dancing is a prayer

and love beats the devil
and revolution is more than moon dust,
less than catastrophe.

I want to dance
my brothers
my sisters
I want to dance.

Lost Baggage

On good days
some of us believe
we have found
Hemingway's
suitcase of stories
the one he left behind
on that December train
though the case
was probably burned
or tossed into a dump
or maybe
just the pages
were discarded
while the wife
of a lonely porter
used it to store hats
on a trip to see her
dyspeptic mother
a cold afternoon
of fading light
in those last good days
1922

Summer of Love

I watch forgotten movies from 1967
and wonder what sort of underwear
the actresses had on beneath their clothing.
I think of the sweat in their crotches
as they filmed a scene for the tenth or twelfth time
say running along a dirt path or dancing
with a man they pretended to know.
I watch forgotten movies from 1967
and wonder what the actresses
had for breakfast the morning
a particular scene was shot.
I wonder about their real lives
and whether they had children
and the old cars they drove home at night
to their small apartments or their parents' homes
or the last time they made love.
I wonder what they bought at the grocery store
and if they collected things
like candles or stamps or old photographs of the dead.
I wonder about their childhood friendships
the real heartbreaks they suffered or inflicted
the dreams they forgot upon waking

the books they read
or if their nipples were ever swollen with infection.
I wonder if they loved their fathers
or if they snored
or if they masturbated with their fingers
or perhaps a hair brush
or the water coming from
the bathtub spigot.
I wonder if they ever had an exotic pet
say a raccoon or an elk or a Komodo dragon.
I wonder about their pubic hair
because in 1967 everyone had pubic hair
thank God
because the world was still sane.
I watch forgotten movies from 1967
because the women on the screen were just people
just like anyone you might meet
on a bus or in a delicatessen
whether or not they owned a raccoon or an elk
and people still dared in those days
still had dreams
still knew real laughter
still thought tomorrow might save everything
but today was just fine, too.
And you can see it all about them

the beautiful women on the screen
caught as if in amber
but they are old now
many of them dead
and beyond desire in the real world.
But who needs the real world?
1967 is real enough.
Roll film.

Last Call

We have been done to death
in midnight bars
of stale beer and cigarettes
the lot of us
propped up by neon
when we needed the moon
shortchanged by truth
and hope scratched from lies
we played ourselves
like nickels in a familiar jukebox
we of the tribe
all heartsick and laughing
done in by absent love
and slender chance
by friends lost to bad faith
or no faith
death
bad jobs
bad marriages
or no reason at all
we of the tribe
drifting

and done to death in midnight bars
we who would live forever
like everyone
you ever knew
I raise my glass
to us all

It's True

This world once had snow in it
and used car lots
dirty lampshades and photographs
of inspired 1916 Bolsheviks
the world had tigers and punk rock
and drugs to make the young girls
sling sweat and dance dance dance
classy dames with runs in their stockings
drinking cheap whiskey
straight from the bottle
the world had red hair and poets
even Sylvia Plath
just imagine a world with trees
or something beautiful
almost no one remembers
but that's how it was
under these cold and constant stars
such a long time ago

About the Author

Jeff Weddle grew up in Prestonsburg, a small town in the hill country of Eastern Kentucky. He has worked as a public library director, disc jockey, newspaper reporter, Tae Kwon Do teacher, and fry cook, among other things. His latest book, *Comes to This*, was published by Nixes Mate Books. His first book, *Bohemian New Orleans: The Story of the Outsider and Loujon Press* (University Press of Mississippi, 2007), won the Eudora Welty Prize and helped inspire Wayne Ewing's documentary, *The Outsiders of New Orleans: Loujon Press* (Wayne Ewing Films, 2007), for which Weddle served as associate producer. His poems, stories, and essays have appeared in dozens of venues, including the anthologies *Surreal South '13* (Press 53, 2013); *Pressure Press Presents* (Pressure Press, 2014); *Stovepiper* (Stovepiper Books, 1994) and *Mondo Barbie* (St. Martin's Press, 1993). Weddle is the author of a poetry collection, *Betray the Invisible* (OEOCO, 2010), a limited-edition, fine press book handcrafted by master book artist Mary Ann Sampson, and a chapbook of Barbie poems, *Not Another Blonde Joke* (Implosion Press, 1991). He is an associate professor in the School of Library and Information Studies at the University of Alabama.

Nixes Mate Books features small-batch artisanal literature, created by writers that use all 26 letters of the alphabet and then some, honing their craft the time-honored way: one line at a time.

More Nixes Mate titles:
ON BROAD SOUND | Rusty Barnes
KINKY KEEPS THE HOUSE CLEAN | Mari Deweese
SQUALL LINE ON THE HORIZON | Pris Campbell
COMES TO THIS | Jeff Weddle
HITCHHIKING BEATITUDES | Michael McInnis
AIR & OTHER STORIES | Lauren Leja
WAITING FOR AN ANSWER | Heather Sullivan
A WORLD WHERE | Paul Brookes
MY SOUTHERN CHILDHOOD | Pris Campbell
THE PAUL BUNYAN BALLROOM | Bud Backen
CAPP ROAD | Matt Borczon
THE WILLOW HOWL | Lisa Brognano
NIXES MATE REVIEW ANTHOLOGY 2016/17
STARLAND | Jessica Purdy
SMOKEY OF THE MIGRAINES | Michael McInnis

Forthcoming titles from Nixes Mate:
JESUS IN THE GHOST ROOM | Rusty Barnes
LUBBOCK ELECTRIC | Anne Elezabeth Pluto
SHE NEEDS THAT EDGE | Paul Brookes
HE WAS A GOOD FATHER | Mark Borczon

nixesmate.pub/books

www.ingramcontent.com/pod-product-compliance
Lightning Source LLC
Chambersburg PA
CBHW052136010526
44113CB00036B/2274